I'm Reading About

SOUTH DAKOTA

The Mount Rushmore State!

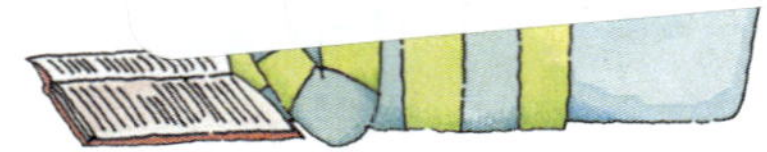

GALLOPADE

by Carole Marsh

Printed and Manufactured in Peachtree City, GA., USA
www.gallopade.com

Book design: John Hanson

Editorial manager: Janice Baker

South Dakota is a great state.

It is one of a kind.

What makes South Dakota special?

Let's read about it and see!

NATIVE AMERICANS

Who lived in South Dakota first?

Native Americans did!

They moved around to find food.
They hunted in South Dakota's woods.
They fished in South Dakota's rivers.
They gathered fruits and seeds and nuts.

EXPLORERS

The first explorers came to South Dakota in 1743. They came from the country of France.

Francois and Louis-Joseph Vérendrye were their leaders. They buried a lead plate in the ground to claim the area for France!

SETTLEMENT

Fort Pierre was the first permanent settlement in South Dakota.
It was named after fur trader Pierre Chouteau.
Fort Pierre was a trading post.
Native Americans and settlers traded furs and other goods.

Fort Pierre was the fur-trading capital of the Northwest in the mid 1800s!

Fort Pierre

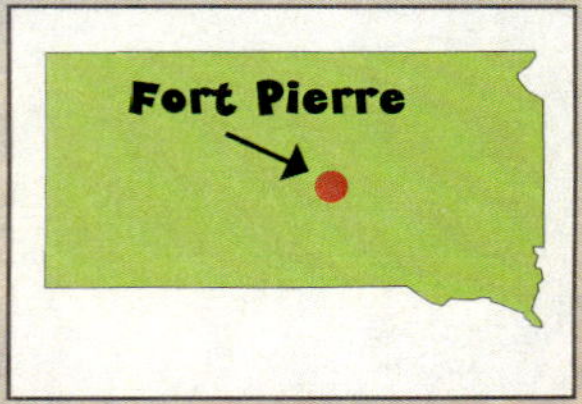

STATEHOOD

South Dakota was the 40th state
to join the United States of America!

Isn't it great,
to be a state!
I bet South Dakota
could hardly wait!

South Dakota became a state in 1889.

South Dakota
The 40th State
Here we are!

FLAG

I am the state flag.
I was adopted in 1992.

What color am I?
I am blue.

Look at me.
What else do you see?

I fly high over the state of South Dakota!

SOUTH DAKOTA
THE MOUNT RUSHMORE STATE
STATE OF SOUTH DAKOTA
UNDER GOD THE PEOPLE RULE
GREAT SEAL
1889

CAPITAL

Say hello to Pierre,
the capital city of South Dakota!

There is an important building in Pierre.
It is the State Capitol.
South Dakota's laws are made there!

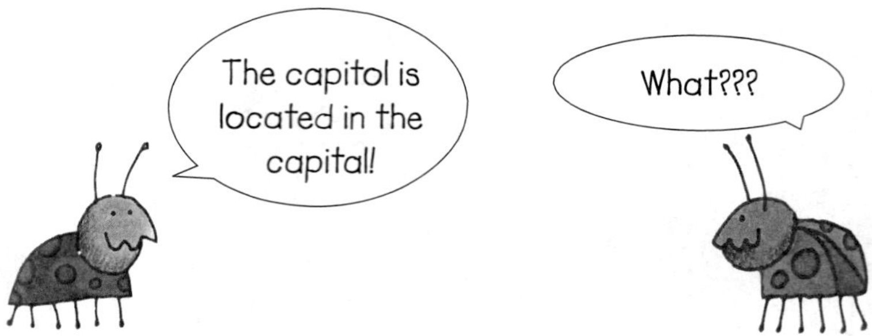

Pierre
Pierre
Capital

SEAL

I am a seal,
but I am not the State Seal.
If I were, I would be very important.
I would be stamped on many official papers.
(Ouch, that might hurt!)

STATE OF SOUTH DAKOTA
UNDER GOD THE PEOPLE RULE
GREAT SEAL
1889

Now, that's official!

NICKNAME

State nicknames are fun!
State nicknames are great!
They share fun facts
about each state!

South Dakota's nickname is "The Mount Rushmore State."

Mount Rushmore is located near Keystone, South Dakota!

The Mount Rushmore State

BORDERS

Look at South Dakota.
South Dakota is in a region called "the Midwest."

South Dakota borders six other states.
Find them on the map!

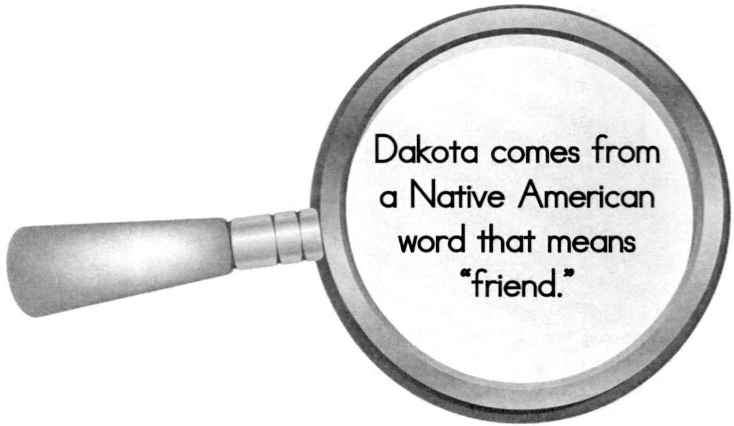

Borders

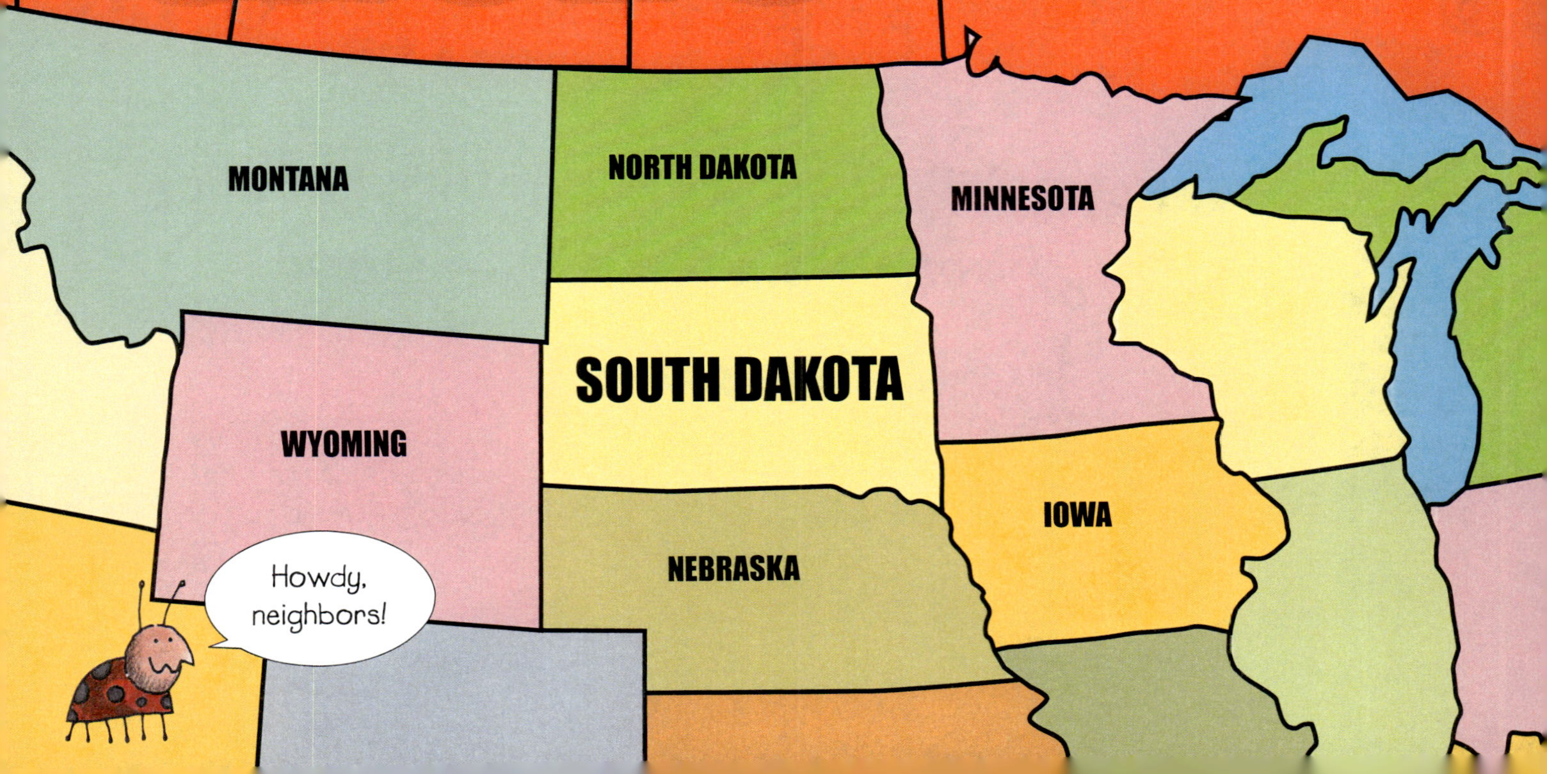
CANADA
MONTANA
NORTH DAKOTA
MINNESOTA
SOUTH DAKOTA
WYOMING
IOWA
NEBRASKA
Howdy, neighbors!

COUNTIES

South Dakota is divided into 66 counties.
Counties are a form of local government.
Counties provide services that people need!
Those services include:

Schools **Parks** **Libraries** **Police**
Firefighters **and More!**

Counties

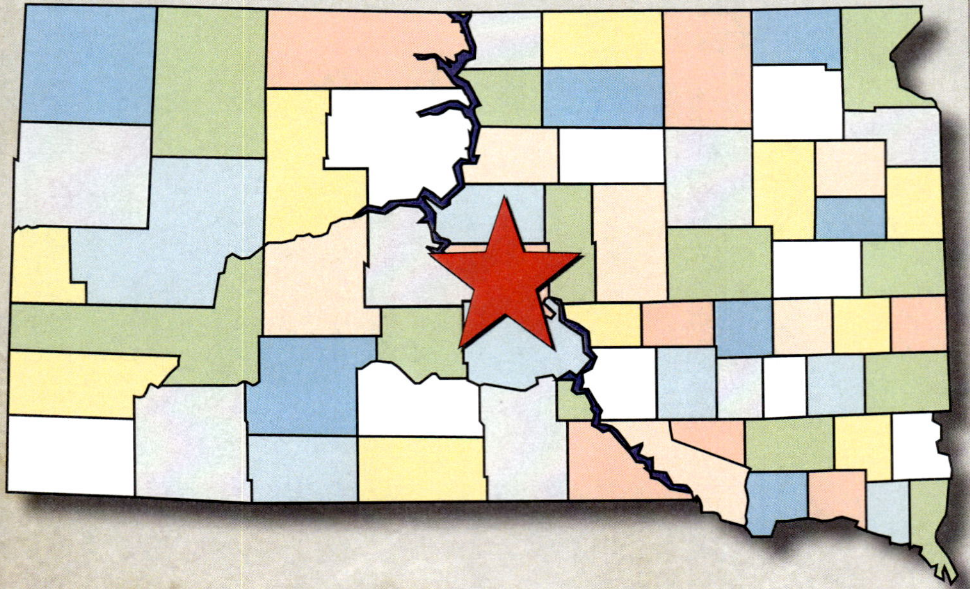

PEOPLE

Many famous people

Crazy Horse
Oglala Lakota Chief

Laura Ingalls Wilder
Author of
Little House on the Prairie

Hubert Humphrey
Vice President of the United States under President Lyndon Johnson

call our state home!

Let's hang out!

Billy Mills

Runner who was the second Native American to win an Olympic gold medal

Mary Hart

Television host and businesswoman

Charles Gemar

NASA astronaut who has flown 3 Space Shuttle missions

Chinese Ring-necked Pheasant

I am the state bird, and I fly
over South Dakota, proud and high.

As I fly, up in the sky,
I flap my wings to tell you "Hi!"

The South Dakota state bird is the
Chinese Ring-necked Pheasant.

BIRD

Pasque

FLOWER

I am the Pasque.
I am the state flower.

I grow where it's warm and sunny.
I bloom in early spring.
I help make South Dakota beautiful!

Look at me! But be careful!
I am poisonous!

Black Hills Spruce

I am a Black Hills Spruce—I'm the state tree.
All over South Dakota is where to find me.

My roots run deep, they keep me strong.
My leaves stay green, all year long.

I stand up straight, big and tall.
Don't climb too high—it would hurt to fall!

TREE

Honeybee

I am the Honeybee.
I am the state insect.

I might sting you if you bother me.
But really, I am your friend.

I carry pollen from flower to flower.
I make honey.
I help South Dakota crops grow.

BZZZZZZZZZZZZ!

INSECT

Prairies

PRAIRIES

Let's go to the prairie!

South Dakota is covered in prairies.
The tall golden grass sways in the breeze.

The prairie is flat and there are no trees.
It stretches as far as the eye can see!

South Dakota's prairies are home to many animals:

Prairie Dogs **Badgers** **Coyotes** **Bison** **Deer** **and More!**

Black Hills

MOUNTAINS

South Dakota's Black Hills are the place to be.
Hiking, fishing, camping—
fun for you and me.

Winter weather brings lots of snow.
Temperatures drop to freezing and below!

Rivers

RIVERS

South Dakota has many rivers.
People like to use rivers for boating and fishing!

This habitat is home to many animals:

Birds Deer Snakes Frogs Fish and More!

Many of South Dakota's early settlers built towns along rivers.

Badlands National Park
Why do they call this the Badlands?
Looks like good land to me!

Badlands National Park is located in southwestern South Dakota.
It is a land of deep canyons, rugged buttes, and grass prairie.
Badlands National Park is a beautiful place!

The largest animal in the park is the American bison.
A bison can be more than 6 feet tall!

LANDMARK

South Dakota Crops

South Dakota has many farms.
Why?
Because South Dakota has good soil
and a mild climate!

Some of the top crops grown in South Dakota are:

Wheat **Corn** **Soybeans** **Sunflowers**

Sports in South Dakota

SPORTS

Baseball! Basketball! Hockey! Football!
South Dakota has it all.

Whether you like to watch or play,
You are sure to have a ball!

Coyotes

Jackrabbits

& More!

South Dakota: Home of Mount Rushmore

Mount Rushmore is in the Black Hills.
It is a huge sculpture carved into the side of a mountain.
The sculpture was carved to honor four of America's great presidents.

Those presidents are:

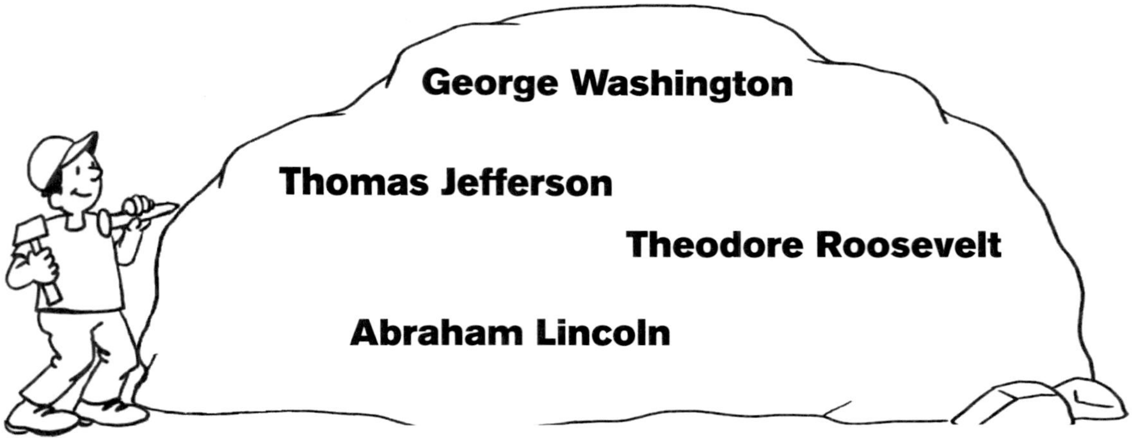

GLOSSARY

butte: a type of hill with a flat top and steep sides

climate: weather conditions in an area over a long period of time

habitat: a place where plants or animals naturally live

laws: rules made by the government

poisonous: something that can cause sickness or death when entering the body

pollen: a yellow powder that helps plants make new plants

region: an area that has similar characteristics

sculpture: a piece of art that is made by carving or molding clay, metal, stone, etc.